We Can Do It!

We Can Do It!

WORDS FROM AWESOME WOMEN

summersdale

WE CAN DO IT!

First published as WOMEN IN THEIR OWN WORDS in 2016

This revised edition © Summersdale Publishers Ltd, 2016

Summersdale Publishers Ltd
46 West Street
Chichester
West Sussex
PO19 1RP
UK

www.summersdale.com

Printed and bound in the Czech Republic

ISBN: 978-1-84953-961-6

INTRODUCTION

Words have the power to change our lives. This book brings together the thoughts of great writers, political pioneers, enchanting actors, historical wits, successful entrepreneurs, modern pop stars, passionate feminists and champions of human dignity — all of them female, and all of them with unique insights to share. No matter when or where they originated, these are words to empower us right now, and to inspire us wherever we go.

There are two ways of spreading light: to be the candle or the mirror that reflects it.

EDITH WHARTON

NO ONE CAN MAKE YOU FEEL INFERIOR WITHOUT YOUR CONSENT.

ELEANOR ROOSEVELT

ONE CHILD, ONE TEACHER, ONE PEN AND ONE BOOK CAN CHANGE THE WORLD.

MALALA YOUSAFZAI

I don't want other people to decide who I am. I want to decide that for myself.

EMMA WATSON

GENTLE LADIES, YOU WILL REMEMBER TILL OLD AGE WHAT WE DID TOGETHER IN OUR BRILLIANT YOUTH!

SAPPHO

We all have our imperfections.
But I'm human, and you know, it's
important to concentrate on other
qualities besides outer beauty.

BEYONCÉ

Try to be a rainbow in someone's cloud.

MAYA ANGELOU

USE EACH INTERACTION TO BE THE BEST, MOST POWERFUL VERSION OF YOURSELF.

MARIANNE WILLIAMSON

YOU HAVE TO BELIEVE IN YOURSELF WHEN NO ONE ELSE DOES — THAT MAKES YOU A WINNER RIGHT THERE.

VENUS WILLIAMS

THE CONTROL AND UNDERSTANDING OF OUR PERSONAL FEARS IS ONE OF THE MOST IMPORTANT UNDERTAKINGS OF OUR LIVES.

HELEN MIRREN

**If I waited for perfection...
I would never write a word.**

MARGARET ATWOOD

WOMEN ARE THE LARGEST UNTAPPED RESERVOIR OF TALENT IN THE WORLD.

HILLARY CLINTON

LIFE APPEARS TO ME TOO SHORT TO BE SPENT IN NURSING ANIMOSITY, OR REGISTERING WRONGS.

CHARLOTTE BRONTË

Never regret. If it's good, it's wonderful. If it's bad, it's experience.

ELEANOR HIBBERT

I think you should take your job seriously, but not yourself – that is the best combination.

JUDI DENCH

THE IMPORTANT THING IS NOT WHAT THEY THINK OF ME, BUT WHAT I THINK OF THEM.

QUEEN VICTORIA

I WANT TO TELL ANY YOUNG GIRL OUT THERE WHO'S A GEEK,

I WAS A REALLY SERIOUS GEEK IN HIGH SCHOOL. IT WORKS OUT.

SHERYL SANDBERG

LIFE IS A SUCCESSION OF LESSONS WHICH MUST BE LIVED TO BE UNDERSTOOD.

HELEN KELLER

Everyone's dream can come true if you just stick to it and work hard.

SERENA WILLIAMS

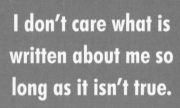

I don't care what is written about me so long as it isn't true.

DOROTHY PARKER

EACH PERSON MUST LIVE THEIR LIFE AS A MODEL FOR OTHERS.

ROSA PARKS

My fears came true: people called me fat and hideous, and I lived. And now I keep living.

LENA DUNHAM

I KNOW I HAVE THE BODY BUT OF A WEAK AND FEEBLE WOMAN; BUT I HAVE THE HEART AND STOMACH OF A KING, AND OF A KING OF ENGLAND TOO.

QUEEN ELIZABETH I

YOU DON'T GET SOMETHING FOR NOTHING AND YOU HAVE TO WORK HARD FOR WHAT YOU WANT IN LIFE.

SARAH STOREY

If you don't like something, change it. If you can't change it, change your attitude. Don't complain.

MAYA ANGELOU

I WOULD VENTURE TO GUESS THAT ANON, WHO WROTE SO MANY POEMS WITHOUT SIGNING THEM, WAS OFTEN A WOMAN.

VIRGINIA WOOLF

YOU'RE ONLY YOUNG ONCE, BUT YOU CAN BE IMMATURE FOREVER.

GERMAINE GREER

Above all, be the heroine of your life, not the victim.

NORA EPHRON

THE MOST COMMON WAY

PEOPLE GIVE UP THEIR POWER

IS BY THINKING THEY

DON'T HAVE ANY.

ALICE WALKER

EVERY MAN I MEET WANTS TO PROTECT ME. I CAN'T FIGURE OUT WHAT FROM.

MAE WEST

LIFE IS EITHER A DARING ADVENTURE OR NOTHING.

HELEN KELLER

SOMEBODY'S NEGATIVITY DUMPED ON YOU IS A BIGGER COMMENTARY ON HOW THEY FEEL ABOUT THEMSELVES THAN YOU.

KELLY RIPA

TAKE ADVANTAGE OF EVERY OPPORTUNITY THAT COMES YOUR WAY, WITH GRACE AND HUMILITY.

BE A SPONGE —
AND ABSORB
AND LEARN.

CHITA RIVERA

SPEAK! IT'S A REVOLUTION FOR WOMEN TO HAVE VOICES.

JILL SOLOWAY

Don't play a supporting role in your own life.

ROBIN ROBERTS

The trouble with some women is they get all excited about nothing – and then they marry him.

CHER

A FEMINIST IS ANYONE WHO RECOGNISES THE EQUALITY AND FULL HUMANITY OF WOMEN AND MEN.

GLORIA STEINEM

I do not wish [women]
to have power over men;
but over themselves.

MARY WOLLSTONECRAFT

WHEN A WOMAN BECOMES

HER OWN BEST FRIEND

LIFE IS EASIER.

DIANE VON FÜRSTENBERG

FITTING IN IS BORING. BUT IT TAKES YOU NEARLY YOUR WHOLE LIFE TO WORK THAT OUT.

CLARE BALDING

Nothing in life is to be feared, it is only to be understood. Now is the time to understand more, so that we may fear less.

MARIE CURIE

IT'S BETTER TO LOOK AHEAD AND PREPARE THAN TO LOOK BACK AND REGRET.

JACKIE JOYNER-KERSEE

TREATING WOMEN WITH RESPECT SHOULD NOT BE CONTINGENT ON WHETHER OR NOT IT 'GETS YOU SOMEWHERE'.

LINDY WEST

You don't know a woman until you have had a letter from her.

ADA LEVERSON

I NEVER LOSE SIGHT OF THE FACT THAT JUST BEING IS FUN.

KATHARINE HEPBURN

IN A TIME OF DESTRUCTION, CREATE SOMETHING.

MAXINE HONG KINGSTON

LOVE AND KINDNESS GO HAND IN HAND.

MARIAN KEYES

Women, like men, should try to do the impossible. And when they fail, their failure should be a challenge to others.

AMELIA EARHART

ONE HOUR OF RIGHT-DOWN LOVE IS WORTH AN AGE OF DULLY LIVING ON.

APHRA BEHN

THE MORE YOU PRACTISE, THE BETTER.

BUT IN ANY CASE, PRACTISE MORE THAN YOU PLAY.

BABE DIDRIKSON ZAHARIAS

YOUR VICTORY IS RIGHT AROUND THE CORNER. NEVER GIVE UP.

NICKI MINAJ

We are not interested in
the possibilities of defeat;
they do not exist.

QUEEN VICTORIA

Dare to be as physically robust and varied as you always were.

SUSIE ORBACH

I DON'T FOCUS ON WHAT I'M UP AGAINST. I FOCUS ON MY GOALS AND I TRY TO IGNORE THE REST.

VENUS WILLIAMS

Personal size and mental sorrow have certainly no necessary proportions. A large bulky figure has as good a right to be in deep affliction, as the most graceful set of limbs in the world.

JANE AUSTEN

BE BRUTALLY FRANK WITH

YOURSELF. IT'S SAFER.

NELLIE BLY

WE ARE THE HERO OF OUR OWN STORY.

MARY McCARTHY

We ask ourselves, 'Who am I to be brilliant, gorgeous, talented, fabulous?' Actually, who are you not to be?

MARIANNE WILLIAMSON

MANY RECEIVE ADVICE, ONLY THE WISE PROFIT FROM IT.

HARPER LEE

LIFE SHRINKS OR EXPANDS IN PROPORTION TO ONE'S COURAGE.

ANAÏS NIN

Lock up your libraries if you like;
but there is no gate, no lock,
no bolt that you can set upon
the freedom of my mind.

VIRGINIA WOOLF

IT'S ABOUT FOCUSING ON THE FIGHT AND NOT THE FRIGHT.

ROBIN ROBERTS

IT IS NOT GOOD TO CROSS THE BRIDGE BEFORE YOU GET TO IT.

JUDI DENCH

MEMORIES OF OUR LIVES, OF OUR WORKS AND OUR DEEDS WILL CONTINUE IN OTHERS.

ROSA PARKS

Love largely and hate nothing.
Hold no aim that does not
chord with universal good.

ELLA WHEELER WILCOX

OBTAIN POWER, THEN, BY ALL MEANS; POWER IS THE LAW OF MAN; MAKE IT YOURS.

MARIA EDGEWORTH

I THINK ONE'S FEELINGS WASTE THEMSELVES IN WORDS;

THEY OUGHT ALL TO BE DISTILLED INTO ACTIONS, AND INTO ACTIONS WHICH BRING RESULTS.

FLORENCE NIGHTINGALE

REAL EDUCATION SHOULD EDUCATE US OUT OF SELF INTO SOMETHING FAR FINER; INTO A SELFLESSNESS WHICH LINKS US WITH ALL HUMANITY.

NANCY ASTOR

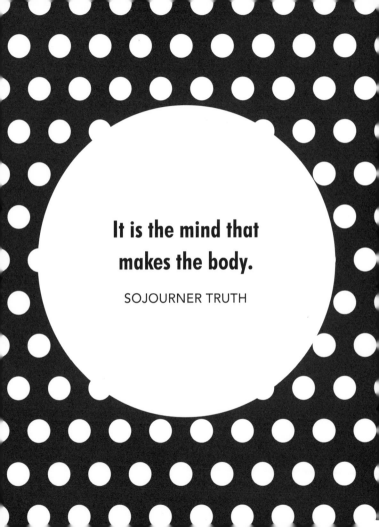

It is the mind that
makes the body.

SOJOURNER TRUTH

**Though he had
Eden to live in, man
cannot be happy alone.**

JOSEPHINE POLLARD

YOU MAY NOT CONTROL ALL THE EVENTS THAT HAPPEN TO YOU, BUT YOU CAN DECIDE NOT TO BE REDUCED BY THEM.

MAYA ANGELOU

**Not many men have
both good fortune
and good sense.**

MARILYN FRENCH

DON'T SPEND TIME BEATING
ON A WALL, HOPING TO
TRANSFORM IT INTO A DOOR.

COCO CHANEL

DON'T BE LIKE ANYONE ELSE. FIND YOUR VOICE, YOUR SCRIPT, YOUR RHYTHMS.

JILL SOLOWAY

Love is an indescribable sensation – perhaps a conviction, a sense of certitude.

JOYCE CAROL OATES

THAT PERFECT
TRANQUILLITY OF LIFE,
WHICH IS NOWHERE TO BE
FOUND BUT IN RETREAT,
A FAITHFUL FRIEND AND
A GOOD LIBRARY.

APHRA BEHN

VIRTUE CAN ONLY FLOURISH AMONGST EQUALS.

MARY WOLLSTONECRAFT

ENERGY RIGHTLY APPLIED AND DIRECTED WILL ACCOMPLISH ANYTHING.

NELLIE BLY

A WORD AFTER A WORD AFTER A WORD IS POWER.

MARGARET ATWOOD

NOT KNOWING WHEN THE DAWN WILL COME, I OPEN EVERY DOOR.

EMILY DICKINSON

**Feminism is the
ability to choose what
you want to do.**

NANCY REAGAN

THE FIRST PROBLEM FOR ALL OF US, MEN AND WOMEN, IS NOT TO LEARN, BUT TO UNLEARN.

GLORIA STEINEM

BEAUTY IS PERFECT IN ITS IMPERFECTIONS,

SO YOU JUST HAVE TO GO WITH THE IMPERFECTIONS.

DIANE VON FÜRSTENBERG

THERE CAN BE NO HAPPINESS IF THE THINGS WE BELIEVE IN ARE DIFFERENT FROM THE THINGS WE DO.

FREYA STARK

Nobility, without virtue, is a fine setting without a gem.

JANE PORTER

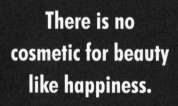

There is no
cosmetic for beauty
like happiness.

MARGUERITE GARDINER

IN SCIENCE, ALL ACTS, NO MATTER HOW TRIVIAL OR BANAL, ENJOY DEMOCRATIC EQUALITY.

MARY McCARTHY

**You can't win them all –
but you can try.**

BABE DIDRIKSON ZAHARIAS

ALL ADVENTURES, ESPECIALLY
INTO NEW TERRITORY,
ARE SCARY.

SALLY RIDE

YOUR SELF-WORTH IS DEFINED BY YOU. YOU DON'T HAVE TO DEPEND ON SOMEONE TELLING YOU WHO YOU ARE.

BEYONCÉ

Suddenly when one has almost made up one's mind to a certain action it casually throws an opportunity into one's path.

ELEANOR HIBBERT

**DO YOUR THING
AND DON'T CARE
IF THEY LIKE IT.**

TINA FEY

THE TRICK IN LIFE IS LEARNING HOW TO DEAL WITH IT.

HELEN MIRREN

All I can do is follow my instincts, because I'll never please everyone.

EMMA WATSON

THERE IS NO CHARM EQUAL
TO TENDERNESS OF HEART.

JANE AUSTEN

GIVE BACK IN SOME WAY. ALWAYS BE THOUGHTFUL OF OTHERS.

JACKIE JOYNER-KERSEE

IT IS JUSTICE, NOT CHARITY, THAT IS WANTING IN THE WORLD.

MARY WOLLSTONECRAFT

OPTIMISM CAN
BE RELEARNT.

MARIAN KEYES

THERE MUST BE A BATTLE, A BRAVE BOISTEROUS BATTLE, WITH PENNANTS WAVING AND CANNON ROARING,

BEFORE THERE CAN BE PEACEFUL TREATIES AND ENTHUSIASTIC SHAKING OF HANDS.

MARY ELIZABETH BRADDON

CEASE TELLING OTHER HUMAN BEINGS WHAT THEY 'SHOULD' AND 'SHOULDN'T' DO WITH THEIR BODIES.

LINDY WEST

Attitude is everything.

DIANE VON FÜRSTENBERG

I never hanker after the past – I prefer to devote myself to new tasks.

STEFFI GRAF

IF YOU OBEY ALL THE RULES, YOU MISS ALL THE FUN.

KATHARINE HEPBURN

I DECLARE TO YOU THAT WOMAN MUST NOT DEPEND UPON THE PROTECTION OF MAN, BUT MUST BE TAUGHT TO PROTECT HERSELF, AND THERE I TAKE MY STAND.

SUSAN B. ANTHONY

In order to be
irreplaceable one must
always be different.

COCO CHANEL

IF EVERYTHING WAS PERFECT, YOU WOULD NEVER LEARN AND YOU WOULD NEVER GROW.

BEYONCÉ

I think if you feel like you
were born to write, then
you probably were.

LENA DUNHAM

NOTHING IS IMPOSSIBLE; THE WORD ITSELF SAYS 'I'M POSSIBLE'!

AUDREY HEPBURN

FORGIVENESS IS A VIRTUE OF THE BRAVE.

INDIRA GANDHI

We must believe that we are gifted for something, and that this thing, at whatever cost, must be attained.

MARIE CURIE

YOU CAN BE STRONG AND TRUE TO YOURSELF WITHOUT BEING RUDE OR LOUD.

PAULA RADCLIFFE

WE SHOULD ALL START TO LIVE BEFORE WE GET TOO OLD. FEAR IS STUPID. SO ARE REGRETS.

MARILYN MONROE

I HAVE LEARNED
OVER THE YEARS
THAT WHEN ONE'S
MIND IS MADE UP, THIS
DIMINISHES FEAR.

ROSA PARKS

I AM NOT BOUND TO GIVE REASONS FOR WHAT I DO TO ANYBODY.

LADY HESTER STANHOPE

LIFE-FULFILLING WORK IS NEVER ABOUT THE MONEY –

WHEN YOU FEEL TRUE PASSION FOR SOMETHING, YOU INSTINCTIVELY FIND WAYS TO NURTURE IT.

EILEEN FISHER

THE MOST
EFFECTIVE WAY TO
DO IT IS TO DO IT.

AMELIA EARHART

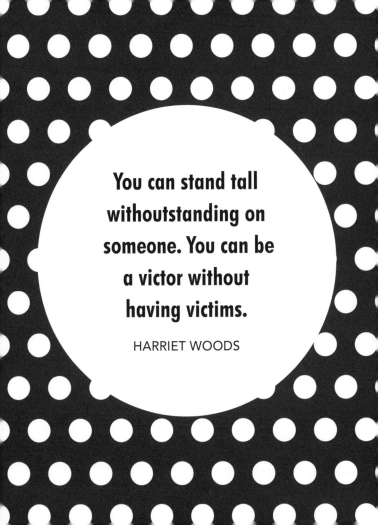

You can stand tall withoutstanding on someone. You can be a victor without having victims.

HARRIET WOODS

Think like a queen.
A queen is not afraid to fail.
Failure is another stepping
stone to greatness.

OPRAH WINFREY

WOMEN NEED REAL MOMENTS OF SOLITUDE AND SELF-REFLECTION TO BALANCE OUT HOW MUCH OF OURSELVES WE GIVE AWAY.

BARBARA DE ANGELIS

The great marriages are partnerships. It can't be a great marriage without being a partnership.

HELEN MIRREN

THE CONNECTIONS BETWEEN AND AMONG WOMEN ARE THE MOST FEARED, THE MOST PROBLEMATIC, AND THE MOST POTENTIALLY TRANSFORMING FORCE ON THE PLANET.

ADRIENNE RICH

SOME OF US ARE BECOMING THE MEN WE WANTED TO MARRY.

GLORIA STEINEM

They say that women talk too much. If you have worked in Congress you know that the filibuster was invented by men.

CLARE BOOTHE LUCE

IT IS THE ULTIMATE LUXURY TO COMBINE PASSION AND CONTRIBUTION. IT'S ALSO A VERY CLEAR PATH TO HAPPINESS.

SHERYL SANDBERG

MY CHOICE, MY RESPONSIBILITY. WIN OR LOSE, ONLY I HOLD THE KEY TO MY DESTINY.

ELAINE MAXWELL

When the whole world is silent, even one voice becomes powerful.

MALALA YOUSAFZAI

YET IF A WOMAN NEVER LETS HERSELF GO, HOW WILL SHE EVER KNOW HOW FAR SHE MIGHT HAVE GOT?

GERMAINE GREER

I AM NO BIRD; AND NO NET ENSNARES ME; I AM A FREE HUMAN BEING WITH AN INDEPENDENT WILL.

CHARLOTTE BRONTË

TAKING JOY IN LIFE IS A WOMAN'S BEST COSMETIC.

ROSALIND RUSSELL

TO SUCCEED YOU HAVE TO BELIEVE IN SOMETHING WITH SUCH A PASSION THAT IT BECOMES A REALITY.

ANITA RODDICK

FAR AWAY THERE IN THE SUNSHINE ARE MY HIGHEST ASPIRATIONS.

I MAY NOT REACH THEM, BUT I CAN LOOK UP AND SEE THEIR BEAUTY, BELIEVE IN THEM, AND TRY TO FOLLOW WHERE THEY LEAD.

LOUISA MAY ALCOTT

A WOMAN WITH A VOICE IS BY DEFINITION A STRONG WOMAN. BUT THE SEARCH TO FIND THAT VOICE CAN BE REMARKABLY DIFFICULT.

MELINDA GATES

How wonderful it is that nobody need wait a single moment before starting to improve the world.

ANNE FRANK

There's power in looking silly and not caring that you do.

AMY POEHLER

I DWELL IN

POSSIBILITY.

EMILY DICKINSON

The giving of love is an education in itself.

ELEANOR ROOSEVELT

YOU MUST FIRST BE WHO
YOU REALLY ARE, THEN
DO WHAT YOU NEED TO
DO, IN ORDER TO HAVE
WHAT YOU WANT.

MARGARET YOUNG

ATTEMPT THE
IMPOSSIBLE
IN ORDER TO
IMPROVE YOUR
WORK.

BETTE DAVIS

You can break that big plan into small steps and take the first step right away.

INDIRA GANDHI

NEVER GIVE UP, FOR THAT IS JUST THE PLACE AND TIME THAT THE TIDE WILL TURN.

HARRIET BEECHER STOWE

FOREVER IS COMPOSED OF NOWS.

EMILY DICKINSON

Every great dream begins with a dreamer. Always remember, you have within you the strength, the patience, and the passion to reach for the stars to change the world.

HARRIET TUBMAN

CHOOSE PEOPLE

WHO LIFT YOU UP.

MICHELLE OBAMA

If you're interested in finding out more about our books, find us on Facebook at **Summersdale Publishers** and follow us on Twitter at **@Summersdale**.

www.summersdale.com